Printed in Austria
for the
strian Federal Government

DATE ~~LOANED~~ DUE

16 Nov '58 A T

Dec 10—58 Enohht

7 Aug '59 J N

25 May '64 AK

16 Jun '64 F H

7 Jul '64 M R

31 Jul '64 R DS

17 NOV '65 DS

11 APR '66 MK

1 8 MAY '66 B M

2 5 FEB '67 MK

4 NOV 1970 K O

2 5 NOV 1970 NM

1 6 DEC 1970 NM

27 AK KO

AUSTRIA IN COLOR

KURT PETER KARFELD

AUSTRIA IN COLOR

TEXT BY
GORDON SHEPHERD

PRINTED AND PUBLISHED BY
ÖSTERREICHISCHE STAATSDRUCKEREI, VIENNA

THE PATTERN OF AUSTRIA

The country which this book brings to life has sat for one thousand years on the busiest crossroads of Europe. Armies, both Christian and heathen, have rolled across it in battle. Great migrations of peoples have spilled over its frontiers. The trade routes and the cultures of a continent have met here, clashed here, and finally joined hands. There has often been equilibrium, but there has never been rest.

This is the key to all things Austrian. To understand the land and its people, the visitor must seek and find this shifting quicksilver balance in the Austrians' art, their architecture, their politics, and even in their food, their dress, and their language.

Each people has at least one characteristic mark which stamps their approach to life, a mark which has been moulded by their particular history as a nation. It is reserve which dominates the British character, and it is Britain's life as an island race which has produced this mood of detachment. It is the desire for novelty and new horizons which stamps the American approach, and the fairly recent pioneer origin of the American people is the main-spring of this urge. With the Austrians, the central theme is compromise, a theme dictated for them by their geographical exposure which, for centuries, has compelled them to absorb the unfamiliar and to come to terms with the intruder. The Austrian may not have been born with this gift. But he was forced to develop it. His character is, in the truest sense, the reflection of his past and the image of his present.

Austrian baroque architecture—that happy fusion of northern solidity and southern fantasy—is often quoted as the classic expression of this Austrian compromise in practice. But it is only one example typical of many. The palaces, castles, monasteries, and churches shown in the following pictures all have a main theme which holds good for the Austrian nation as a whole—to create and to survive by adaptation.

The combination of old and new which results is, of course, in no way an Austrian prerogative. All ancient countries are forced to dress up their present alongside their past. Indeed, Rome and Athens, whose classical ruins slumber alongside the luxury hotels, are better examples of such contrasts than Vienna, where modern architecture has so far done little to transform the traditional face of the town.

But the unique Austrian achievement has been to preserve the old character amid the new setting. The Romans and Greeks of today are no longer the peoples whom Augustus and Pericles ruled. But the Viennese, one feels, have remained essentially the same folk with that same gentle and insidious philosophy which sweetened life for Caesar's garrison legions in Vindobona, the Vienna of nearly 2,000 years ago. The result of this happy gift is that even those things which the Austrians have copied from their neighbours take on a specifically Austrian character. Thus even Austrian baroque architecture itself, though based on foreign inspiration, could only exist in the form which the Austrians gave it amidst their own countryside. The Austrian pattern is not just the passive mixture of alien colours. It is the blending of the rose-grower who, from the shoots of two or three blossoms will bring to life a new flower, with a vitality and a character all of its own.

The pictures which follow were certainly not selected deliberately to show that Austrian universality which has also come from her "crossroads history". But even without intention, many examples appear in these pages—Belvedere Palace in Vienna, the home of a European as well as an

Austrian soldier; Dürnstein Castle in the Wachau, where an English king captured on his return from the Crusades was held for one of the fattest ransoms of the Middle Ages; Bernstein in the Burgenland, the best preserved of a long chain of fortresses which once formed the frontline of the Christian world against the heathen east; the fairy tale castle of Hochosterwitz in Carinthia, whose very spelling shows the trace of a long-vanished Celtic occupation; Beethoven's house among the vineyards of Vienna, and Haydn's church on the edge of the Hungarian plain, monuments to two of the giants of world music who lived and worked in Austria; and finally Salzburg where, once a year, the world still comes to hear their compositions amid the works of Mozart, Austria's special son.

The Austrian countryside as depicted here typifies as much as the buildings the lesson of her history—dividing and at the same time blending the different streams of European culture and commerce. Two great themes run through these landscape pictures. They are the Danube and the Alps: Europe's longest river and Europe's greatest mountain range. It is along this river since time immemorial that the merchandise of East and West have been exchanged and the inland fleets of peace and war have sailed. And it is through the lovely valleys which vertically pierce the Austrian Alps that the caravans of the north have moved down to the Mediterranean shores since the earliest trading times. Better than any words or dates, the banks of this river and the passes of these mountains illustrate the destiny which the Austrian people have been called on to fulfil.

But these landscape pictures can tell us even more. The Austrian provinces are not only one of the vital connecting links of Europe's commerce and communications. They are also, geologically and botanically, a transition ground from west to east, and from north to south. This is true of Austria's mountains, her plains, and her lakes. The

Tyrolean Alps, majestic though they are, are set in a minor key to the even mightier peaks of Switzerland, and it is in Austria that this great range tails off eastwards in countless minor chains until it finally dies away in the soft hills of the woods which overlook the capital. Vienna's famous Kahlenberg is not just a picturesque look-out point. It is also the last spur of that great Alpine massif which rises 500 miles to the west. Similarly, the rich cornfields of Lower Austria and the Burgenland are not merely the bread-basket of Vienna. They are the beginnings of that great Central European plain into which, on Austrian soil, the Alps subside. It is in the Austrian Burgenland, among the squat brown houses of the villages and on the reedy shores of Lake Neusiedl that one can sniff the first melancholy-sweet breath of the "puszta". Even the Austrian lakes form a half-way stage in colour and in temperature between the icy and ice-blue lakes of the north and the warm sapphire waters of Como or Lugano.

If these ageless influences of nature have left their mark on Austria's buildings and her culture, and even on the plants and trees of her countryside, it is obvious that they have also indelibly stamped the character of her people. As a nation, the Austrians are unprejudiced, unenvious, and politically unambitious. The first quality springs from their unbroken contacts over the centuries both with neighbours and with distant intruders belonging to different races and religions.

The other two qualities have sprung, partly from this, but partly also from the violent ups and downs of their own history. The Austrians have held and lost great influence in the councils of the world. They began in the first Millennium as the inhabitants of a small feudal mark, set up by the lords of Bavaria to guard the eastern approaches of Christian Europe—a sort of suicidal outer drawbridge which had to be defended because it could never be raised. It was not until 1156—when the outlines of an integrated nation state had already appeared in France and England—that the Austrians became even a separate dukedom, with some legal independence of their own. Through the acquisition of Styria, Carinthia, Krain, and the Tyrol this inner Austrian dukedom grew gradually into one of the most powerful territorial units of Central Europe. Finally, in the 16th century, and under the leadership of those same Habsburgs who had expanded Austria's basic provinces, the dukedom grew by dynastic marriage and war into one of the greatest European land powers of all time, extending to Burgundy, Spain, Hungary and Bohemia, and crowned with the dignity of the Holy Roman Empire.

This unwieldy complex was divided soon after its formation into a western and an eastern half, ruled respectively from Madrid and Vienna. The eastern part, inadequately called Austro-Hungary, survived intact until the 20th century as the massive guardian of conservatism and stability in Central and Eastern Europe. Then, in 1918, the dynasty, the far-flung provinces, the dignity, the prosperity, and the power disappeared almost overnight. Though weakened by internal tensions, the Empire was destroyed only by war. By November of that year, the Austrian people found themselves territorially back at the same starting point which their ambitious rulers had won for them 500 years before. But now, it was not a strong and rising dukedom which straddled the Enns and the Danube, but a dazed and enfeebled republic, facing a ring of hostile neighbours.

From this painful cycle in their own fortunes the Austrians have learned instinctively to rate the human and the spiritual values of life higher than the political. They have learned indeed what an ungrateful, exhausting and dangerous imposture the search for power can be. It is an attitude which could be of service to a world seeking an alternative to the rule of force.

These same qualities and this same history have made the Austrians—and particularly the Viennese—one of the most receptive of peoples. Theirs is not the mondaine cosmopolitanism which eagerly grasps at any new experience for its own sake and seeks to be Europe's arbiter and pioneer of taste and intellect. Indeed, perhaps because he has absorbed so much in the past, the Austrian of today will hesitate before modifying his own way of life with still more foreign notions. But even those ideas which he is reluctant to copy he is willing to respect. He is glad to have almost anyone enter his country and, once there, prepared to let him argue his case and live his life in peace.

Even as an occupied state in the ten years after the Second World War, Austria's laws of political asylum were exemplary. And despite the tensions of the Cold War in those difficult years and despite the physical pressure of foreign garrisons which stood on opposite sides in that Cold War, the Austrian government managed to have these rights of asylum carried out in practice on its soil. This constant stream of destitute refugees threw a heavy strain on an already stricken Austrian economy. Austria's hospitality was sometimes deliberately misinterpreted and sometimes genuinely misunderstood. Yet the country continued then with its task, and will continue as a free country now, so long as there are refugees who clamour for asylum along its borders. This attitude is remarkable yet understandable. To the Austrians, the political refugees of the twentieth century are just another phase in that constant shifting of peoples which they have had to live with in the Danube Basin for nearly two thousand years. This is the deeper cosmopolitanism. It consists not of imitation but of tolerance.

To some extent, of course, the Austrian's natural sympathy for foreigners is explained by the simple fact that the blood of nearly all the nations of the continent flows in his veins. Almost any European foreigner and certainly any Central European neighbour is the Austrian's "alter ego". The mere list of races who peopled the Austrian lands at the dawn of civilization illustrates this mixture—

Illyrians, Celts, Romans, Teutons, Avars, Slavs, and Magyars, to name only a few. But a big role was also played by political chance, by the fact that for nearly six hundred years, from the late 13th to the early 20th century, the destiny of the Austrian people themselves became entangled and identified with the destiny of that great supra-national empire mentioned above.

The historical accident that, in 1273, the Swabian Count Rudolf assumed the leadership of the then German-speaking world and founded in Vienna the dynasty of the Habsburgs completed the cosmopolitan education of the Austrians. Till then, theirs had been the instinctive universality possessed by all races with mixed blood. But, as the Middle Ages moved into modern times, and that same dynasty still sat and ruled from Vienna, the Austrians learned their universality all over again—from their imperial office desks.

At its zenith, this empire "on which the sun never set" stretched to the borders of the then civilized world: at one end was the warm breath of Madrid and at the other the rough wind of the Asiatic steppes. And, for centuries, the Austrian was the "primus inter pares" of this company, the first member among all this motley family of nations, the people of the same blood and language as the Emperor himself, and therefore his natural choice as servants and administrators. One can compare that old Austria, which many of these photographs depict, to a vast landed estate, run too long on feudal lines, but managed on the whole with benevolence and justice. On this estate, the Austrians became the liveried stewards and game-keepers, stationed in all remote corners of the great property, as well as in Vienna itself, and preoccupied not with any national issues of their own, but rather with the problems of the fifteen different races whom they had to administer.

The fact that they were concerned more with the day-to-day business of empire than with their own fate brings us to another salient feature of the Austrians of today—their late development as a nation-state. It is no coincidence that the pictures in this book contain no national monuments comparable with George Washington's statue or Nelson's Column in London. For the Austrians reached this 20th century without a specifically national history of their own. Nationalism was the force which, throughout the 19th century, threatened the federal structure on which the Empire was built; and the Austrians, as the first servants of the dynasty, could only indulge in it at the cost of disloyalty to their masters. Thus when, in 1918, the great empire of which they had been the ruling instrument collapsed around them, they had to seek for a patriotism of their own on which to start life again as a small republic.

In the relatively short space of time that has passed since, the Austrians have managed, despite a total of seventeen years of foreign occupation, to find this national identity which the Empire unwittingly withheld from them. This has meant shaking off all the nostalgia of imperialism on the one hand, and on the other, the even more difficult task of reducing to proper perspective their relationship with their German cousins in the north. But at last this Austrian people, so old in tradition, have found the one thing which even their long history denied to them—a political personality of their own.

The traditional tolerance of the Austrians as well as their newly developed national identity are two characteristics over which there is little room for dispute or misunderstanding. But many other popular beliefs about them are based on illusions whose persistence is as strange as their origin.

There is, for example, the notion that the Austrians are a lighthearted, feckless people with little or no thought for what tomorrow may bring. In actual fact, their cheerfulness is balanced by an almost equal dose of wistful melancholy, and these two strains are perfectly represented in their music. Austrian music can rightly be taken as the expres-

8

sion of the nation's way of life. But it must be studied in its entirety, and not in those sections which the outside world will persist in substituting for the whole.

The charm and the immortality of Johann Strauss are beyond argument. It is however high time to dispose of the sickly legend that his waltzes form a sort of magic and universal key to both Austria's culture and her character. In some ways, indeed, the Viennese waltz is exceptional rather than typical, and so was the atmosphere in which it was born and in which it flourished.

The Vienna of Johann Strauss's days was a doomed capital living through a sort of false springtime. This was the socalled "Gründerzeit", when a sudden economic boom, based on the first delayed effects of industrialization and a modern credit system, happened to coincide with a lull in those domestic and international conflicts which were soon to tear the empire savagely apart. Strauss was the symbol of this new middle class wealth; the symbol also of this Fata Morgana of Austro-Hungary's political stability, a deceptive vision which was destroyed for all time by the cannons of the First World War. There is nothing novel in this paradox. Other civilizations and other empires have lived through this same sudden blaze of sunshine which comes immediately before the long night.

But the picture of the Austrians which spread to the furthest corners of the earth with Strauss's melodies in the 1870's was particulary misleading. For, as a people, they never have had and they never will have that bursting energy and youthful confidence which vibrates through most (though not all) of these famous tunes. A truer keynote to their character could be heard, even then, in the older musical background of the age — the sad, but good-tempered resignation of Schubert. And, as events were to prove, this also turned out to be a better sign-post of the tragedy lying ahead for Austro-Hungary than the brightly-painted park bandstands of Johann Strauss.

It should be noted, incidentally, that a strong, bitter-sweet undertone also lies beneath the music of Vienna's winegardens, the equally famous "Heurigen Lieder", which have helped to perpetuate the Strauss legend. Taken as a whole, this popular music is far less gay and uninhibited than French or even English drinking songs. Death stalks through the choruses of the Heurigen Lieder as well as life, and as many of their themes are devoted to nostalgia over the past as to contentment over the present. Not that this makes them any the less attractive. They are possibly the best drinking songs in the world, and the Vienna winegarden is certainly the best setting in the world for such music. But this is precisely because both of them cater in equal measure for the twin effects of alcohol—exuberance and melancholy. To dwell only on the gaiety is, in other words, to underestimate Vienna's contribution to the cult of the grape.

So much for the Strauss myth of light-headed gaiety. The illusion about the fecklessness of the Austrians is just as far off the mark. It is true that, politically, Austria's history has left her with a certain fatalism which even her new national spirit has not shaken off. But in their private lives, few people make such earnest and conscientious endeavours to ensure themselves against the hazards of the future as do the Austrians. If they have a mania, it is for security, not for extravagance.

To have a pension to look forward to is the very summit of the Austrian's material desires in life. Out of a total working population of over two million it is estimated that at least three quarters are in pensionable jobs of one sort or another. And no fewer than 760,000 are actually retired and drawing pensions. Not long ago, at an Austrian school in Styria, the teachers conducted an inquiry as to what their pupils wished to do for a living. Among the junior grades, who were unversed in the hard economic facts of life, the most popular career chosen was that of "pensioner". That could only happen in Austria.

This demand for security stretches far outside the ranks of bureaucrats and the like who, in any country, prefer a fixed certainty to a variable uncertainty. In Austria, it pervades also the artistic and commercial world. The typical actor or musician in this country is either state-paid or state-subsidized. Most of the colourful artists and singers of the Vienna Opera are in fact established civil servants with solid pensions to look forward to when their charms begin to fade and their voices no longer reach up to the third gallery.

The same urge for security before adventure stamps the Austrian businessman. Perhaps this comes from his inborn inclination to deadsafe markets such as those his ancestors enjoyed for generations in the old empire. Perhaps it is due to his late contact with the industrial revolution, or to Austria's lack throughout her history of overseas possessions. But whatever the reason, it is the spirit of caution, not the spirit of the gambler which possesses him. He is very often a successful industrialist, as the splendid steel mills, power plants, and textile factories of the country show. But he is rarely a successful salesman. Characteristically enough, his many inventions have, as often as not, been developed by other nations. Risk—that factor on which business in the capitalist world is normally built up — is anathema to the Austrian. And even those who do gamble and win are usually content with the initial prosperity which results. The millionaire bent on doubling his fortune every decade of his life is an unthinkable figure for Austrians. They have no business tycoons; not only because their economy is relatively small but also because their mentality is totally unsuitable. Their aim is an ample sufficiency and not a riotous surplus.

This attitude brings with it a certain lack of enterprise which sometimes handicaps the Austrian on the world stage. But he cherishes a sneaking feeling that his approach is the right one; and the more "manager disease" spreads among the more bustling nations, the more this view is shared elsewhere in the world. For what the Austrian's life loses in excitement and the chance of great wealth, it gains in relaxation and the prospect of solid comfort.

This, more than anything else, is the keynote to the "Gemütlichkeit", that easy-going and good-natured approach to life, for which the Austrian and above all the Viennese is famous. Here is no myth that needs exploding, and no legend that needs correcting. In this respect at least, there is no contrast and no interruption between Austria's imperial past and her republican present. Austrian Gemütlichkeit runs like a bright ribbon even through the tragedies of the nation's life. The ribbon is light in texture but tough, and indestructible because it is so intangible.

Obviously, this Gemütlichkeit must have certain material preconditions. It would be almost unattainable, for example, in a country which did not grow its own wine. Any nation lucky enough to live under the shadow of the grape-vine has a natural warmth which comes harder to those peoples who have to import their sunshine by the bottle from abroad. But even among the quality wine-growing countries of Europe, Austria holds a unique position. She is the only land where, year after year, the people account for virtually the entire crop themselves. The wine output of Austria in 1953, for example, reached the respectable total of 18,174,046 gallons. The Austrians drank the lot—apart from 345,290 gallons, or barely 2%, which went for export.

To transfer this crop from the vineyard to the palate, an impressive retail organization is maintained. Vienna alone has roughly 7,500 establishments at which a glass of wine can be had at any hour of the day, not counting the hundreds of wine-gardens scattered on the wooded outskirts of the city. There are, in fact, few streets anywhere in the capital where it is necessary to walk more than 250 yards with a thirst. And though not as cheap as the fresh air of the Vienna Woods, the open wine of Austria is within the reach of most (as the disposal of the annual crop would indicate). An "Achtel", or a full wine-glass measure, can be had in the modest inns for a few pence. This is an enjoyment whose broad popular base enhances it for all.

Another material factor in this happy philosophy of life is, of course, the physical beauty of the countryside and the ready-made facilities for enjoyment which it offers. Austria is one of those fortunate lands whose attractions are spread liberally over the four seasons: the winter snow of the mountains gives as much joy and sport to native and foreigner alike as the summer sunshine of the lakes and forests. And the result is about the nearest thing to mass but unorganized recreation which any modern society can boast. These relaxations can be indulged in by all classes with all incomes. Here again, we come up against that essential undertone of Austrian life—the happy undertone of pleasures shared and multiplied by the very process of division.

In Vienna too, the traditional Austrian Gemütlichkeit is helped by nature. No capital of the world has a green belt of such depth and unspoilt beauty so close to its concrete heart as Vienna possesses in its famous woods. They encircle the whole north-western approaches to the capital and can be reached, even on the tortoise backs of the city's trams, in less than half an hour's journey from Vienna's centre.

But, in the capital, Nature has also been partly helped by man in building the cradle for a pleasant life. True, Vienna is not lovely in the exotic or romantic style of many another European beauty-spot. Though commonly thought of as the greatest Danubian city and though geographically the centre of the whole Danube basin, it is not even built on the river along which its destiny flows. The Danube near Vienna is, for the most part, a muddy, grey-green waterway, disciplined like a canal with uninspiring artificial banks, and forced to run outside the city proper, through the flood-control area of the eastern plains. Vienna's only "river", the so-called "Wienfluss", is, in fact, a docile trickle of water as shallow as a children's paddling pool, which wanders down one of the city's parks in a special concrete bed ten times as big as itself. All this is aesthetically a loss, as the contrasting arrangement of Prague, Budapest, Florence, Paris and London —to name only a few of Europe's "river-cities"— will show.

Yet, even in this aesthetic loss, there is a specifically Viennese gain. For the very fact that the planners of the city did not allow it to be cut into two by their river meant that the centre of the capital gained in compactness and character. Vienna's "Innere Stadt", that bustling octagon of narrow streets enclosed by the broad Ringstrasse, is one of the most concentrated and self-contained centres to be found in any major city. There is much that is beautiful outside this centre. But the passing stranger who, with only three hours in Vienna to spare, walks carefully through this Inner City will take away with him the unforgettable essence of the capital, even should he never return. Palaces, and at the head of them the old Imperial Hofburg; churches, and above all the Cathedral of St. Stephen's; the cultural shrines of Austria, notably the Burgtheater and the rebuilt Opera itself; museums and monuments from an earlier age and luxury shops and hotels of today: Vienna's past and her present are lovingly pressed together in his tiny space less than two miles across. What other capitals have sprawled, Vienna has thrown into one, behind what were formerly the fortress walls of the medieval town.

The result of this compactness is an intimacy which no other city of such size can boast. The visitor who is receptive to this appeal becomes, in 24 hours, an honorary resident. This is "Gemütlichkeit" in operation and again, it springs from a pleasure shared. Vienna is one of the few sight-seeing capitals of Europe which has no "tourist centre" and no tourist complex.

Its native citizens and its most casual visitors merge naturally into one.

But neither the vineyards of the Kahlenberg and Nussdorf nor the wine gardens all around them; neither the broad spread of the Vienna Woods nor the friendly turmoil of the Inner City could, by themselves, have created the Austrian's philosophy of life. "Gemütlichkeit" is a personal characteristic. The face which it shows to the world may be an anonymous image of a whole capital, a whole people and a whole country. But it is born in the individual. And if it ever perishes, it is in the individual that it must first of all die.

Applied to the tormented world of today, this Austrian way of life becomes an appeal to reason. What it stands for in the political sphere is not the concern of this book. Nor indeed is its political content unique, whatever special qualifications and opportunities Austria may possess. All small nations, pressed between the great power blocks of the world, aim naturally at peaceful reconciliation. But what the Austrian philosophy aims at in the sphere of ordinary social relations is almost unique, at least among the modern industrialized peoples of the world. For, alone among these nations, Austria preaches and practises the philosophy of leisure. Austrian "Gemütlichkeit" is an isolated protest against the paradox of our Machine Age in which man constantly has more time placed at his disposal and yet steadily has less time to spare.

More perhaps than any European people since the Ancients, the Austrian still tries to build his real life around his leisure hours. Here he will show reserves of energy which are astounding. The young Viennese clerk or worker will cheerfully do overtime on a Friday in order to spend Saturday and Sunday on a ski-ing trip to the mountains—standing overnight in a crowded train; and fully prepared on arrival to march up to his chosen peak with a 30 lb. rucksack on his back. The Austrian is not, by disposition, "queue-minded". But he will stand in line with the patience of Job and the tenacity of a mule in the hope of securing a last-minute ticket for a sold-out performance at one of his concert-halls or opera houses.

This love of leisure is not simple hedonism, and it is certainly not pure laziness—the Austrian works steadily enough for his free time, as his remarkably low post-war record for industrial strikes shows. It is rather based upon the instinctive feeling that there is more to life than the amassing of money or the quest for power. "Gemütlichkeit" is an appeal for perspective, relaxation and tolerance in this frantic and vicious age. There could be no greater mistake than to think of its message purely in terms of the wine-garden's conviviality. The Austrian would never think of his own philosophy of life as a crusade. Yet a crusade without banners is, in fact, what it is.

No introduction to Austria and its people, however superficial, would be complete without some account of the provincial basis of the nation's life. Indeed, without this, no introduction would even be intelligible. For Austria is not simply divided into nine parts, as Caesar's Gaul was into three. It is rather the nine separate parts which go to make up Austria.

Despite all the centralization which the machinery of a modern Federal Republic has brought, the ancient provinces remain the real units of Austrian life. They were there, not only before the Republic, but even before the Habsburg dynasty which preceded it. And 20th century parliamentary techniques are as powerless to centralize them out of existence as was the bureaucracy of the Empress Maria Theresia two centuries before. Nor, today, would the attempt be made. Here again, the Austrian has struck his famous balance. Vienna and the provincial capitals have reached a division of labours which works, considering the difficulties, with remarkable harmony, and serves to strengthen the political structure of the Republic as a whole. For the activity and the influence of the provinces, with their contrasting background and character, not only help to preserve what is best in the nation's old traditions. They help also to guarantee what is best in the Republic's new democracy.

The provinces act as an automatic check on the aspirations of each other; and together they act as a counterweight to the supremacy, however loyally acknowledged, of the federal capital. Control is the essence of free government. To some extent, the provinces in their capacity as provinces fulfil this function in Austria more effectively than the National Parliament in Vienna. In a very real sense, therefore, they are the guardians of Austria's future as well as of her past.

For this reason, it is with historical, as well as pictorial justice to Austria that the photographs on these pages should depict each separate component of the Austrian state: Vienna, Lower Austria, Upper Austria, Styria, Carinthia, Salzburg, Tyrol, Vorarlberg and the Burgenland. Their varied character which the pictures show is not only a matter of landscape and geographical position. It is also implicit in the very different circumstances in which they were joined together as the successive pieces of an Alpine jig-saw puzzle; and, not the least, in the span of nearly ten centuries which were needed to achieve this union.

The historical and strategic heart of the whole complex is the area of Lower Austria which surrounds the capital. This was the original "Ostmark" of 976, as established by the Holy Roman Empire and allotted to the Babenbergs to secure the Empire's unsettled flank. It originally stretched only from the River Enns to the upward curve of the Danube near Spitz in the Wachau Valley, but seventy years later the same energetic Babenbergs had already extended their fiefdom eastwards of Vienna to the banks of the River Leitha.

Vienna itself, though first mentioned in documents as early as 881, only assumed its permanent importance for Austria in the early 11th century as the seat of the Babenberg rulers. For nearly 900 years this city remained the centre of the Austrian lands, and for over two-thirds of this enormous span it was also the capital of the Austrian Empire, and the seat of the Habsburg dynasty which succeeded the Babenbergs. Yet here is straight away a typical paradox. Though it is the oldest and most venerable of Austrian possessions, Vienna is juridically the youngest of Austrian provinces: it did not achieve that constitutional status until 1922, perhaps because the earlier centuries had always taken its significance for granted.

One by one, the other provinces of present-day Austria were added to the "heart-lands" of the Habsburg realm: parts of Upper Austria in 1156: Styria in 1192; Carinthia in 1335; Tyrol in 1365; Vorarlberg in 1375; and finally, the spiritual principality of Salzburg in 1805, as compensation for the loss of Tuscany. All these regions were the acquisitions of the dynasty—some by inheritance, some by grant, some by marriage, and some by purchase. Only one was added territorially by the Austrian Republic—the area of Western Hungary which was taken over by Austria in 1921 as the province of the Burgenland.

This long dynastic struggle by which the Austrian people built up their present home explains much in the position of the provinces today. These provinces are nearly as old as the counties of Britain, and have seen even more vicissitudes. Yet they have preserved over the centuries a great deal of the independence which the English counties have long ago lost. This is largely because, until 1918, they were still among the principal administrative units of the Empire, each reflecting in its own government that balance between dynasty on the one hand, and local landowners, industrialists, clergy, craftsmen, and ordinary citizen-voters on the other, which became typical of domestic political life in Austria towards the end of the Habsburg era.

Between 1919 and 1929, the Federal Republic made heavier inroads than the Empire into the authority of the provinces. Apart from the traditional prerogatives such as defence and foreign policy, the capital secured powers of exclusive jurisdiction and internal security, and even the complete control of higher education throughout the country. Yet, despite this, Federal Austria and its different provinces are today still juridically separate bodies and, internally, each province has retained the sole right to administer its sub-districts, as well as keeping certain privileges of local government vis-à-vis the Republic as a whole. In this way, the needs of sovereignty in a modern state have been balanced against the local traditions of the Middle Ages.

The siting of the various provincial capitals reflects their historic role in strategy and commerce. Bregenz, for example, is the gate to the Swiss Alps; Innsbruck to the Italian Alps; Klagenfurt to the Adriatic; and Graz to the great south-eastern hinterland of Yugoslavia and Hungary. Others, like Linz, are among the main road, rail and river junctions of Central Europe; and, in the case of this flourishing Upper Austrian capital, a major industrial city in its own right. It is their independent role as communication centres which give these provincial capitals an importance and a separate vitality which nothing can efface.

Our superficial introduction to the Austrian state and its people can fittingly close with this survey of the provinces. For the rich and varied spectrum of provincial life reflects again the essential pattern of Austria. This country "which God loved" remains the connecting link of a whole continent; and today, the connecting link is made doubly strong because an alloy of old and new has been poured into the metal.

There is the poetry of great events as well as the poetry of beauty in this view of Vienna from the Belvedere Palace. It was down the slopes of the Vienna Woods shown in the distance that, on 12th September 1683, the relief army descended to do battle with the Turks in their great siege of the Austrian capitel. This was in fact a siege of Christendom, and the victory which Austrian and Polish arms gained on that day was a victory for Christendom. It was, incidentally, in this same historic battle that Prince Eugene of Savoy, who later built the Belvedere Palace, began his long career as a European soldier and statesman. He had entered the service of the Austrian army in the year of the Turkish invasion after his services had been refused by Louis XIV of France due to his slight build.

And it was in the same gardens of this Belvedere Park that the Austrian people celebrated their most joyous event as a modern republic. On 15th May 1955 the paths and lawns shown here were covered with tens of thousands of Viennese who had gathered to watch the signature, in the Marble Chamber of the Palace, of the State Treaty which restored to Austria her freedom and identity after seventeen years of foreign occupation.

There is thus a gap of two and a half centuries separating the days, in very different settings, when Eugene of Savoy and the Foreign Ministers of the four great 20th century powers looked from the windows of Belvedere at this view. But the spire of St. Stephen's Cathedral in the foreground and the Vienna Woods on the horizon were there on both occasions.

15

The whole complex of the Belvedere Palace was built between 1714 and 1722 by Lukas von Hildebrandt as a summer residence for the great European soldier, statesman and man of letters Eugene of Savoy. The site chosen was a long sloping meadow just outside the fortifications of the old town. Though the Upper Palace, a glimpse of which is shown here, is normally thought of as Prince Eugene's home, this building was almost entirely used during his lifetime for audiences and banquets. The Prince himself lived in the long, one-storey "Lower Belvedere", a master-piece of intimate baroque architecture which Hildebrandt constructed to the Prince's orders at the foot of the sloping site.

Prince Eugene's Palace stood under no happy star. His heirs ransacked it after his death for everything they could sell, and most of the beautiful furnishings and pictures which the Prince had collected during his lifetime, as well as his irreplaceable private archive, were dispersed. Fortunately, the Palace itself was shortly afterwards acquired by the ruling house of Habsburg.

In the hands of this unhappy dynasty, it lived through some typically tragic moments. Though no one realized it at the time, the most poignant of these was the famous Court Ball and Gala held in the Belvedere in April 1770 to bid farewell to the Austrian Archduchess Maria Antonia two days before her marriage with Louis XVI of France. As Queen Marie Antoinette, she was to die on the scaffold with him 23 years later.

It was not until 1910 that the Belvedere Palace received a permanent royal resident worthy of its style. And even then there was a tragic destiny in the choice. This last inhabitant of the Palace was none other than the Archduke Franz Ferdinand, Heir-Presumptive to the Austrian throne, who was murdered at Sarajewo in June 1914.

16

This house, the so-called "Beethoven House", at Heiligenstadt on the slopes of the Vienna Woods, was lived in by the great composer in 1817. It was one of the many quarters Beethoven took up in the restless years between 1792 and his death in 1827 which he spent in the Austrian capital. No major works were composed in this building, but it was at a house in the Probusgasse a few yards away that the Second Symphony was written in the summer and autumn of 1802.

The name Probusgasse recalls, incidentally, the role which the ancient Romans played in establishing Vienna for all time as a winegrowing centre. It was the Roman Emperor Probus who, in the latter part of the Third Century A. D., authorized his garrison in the province of Noricum, as Roman Austria was then called, to help in constructing the vineyards on the slopes of the Danube.

The wine which Beethoven tasted was the ultimate descendant of these vines, and wine from the same stock can be drunk in this same house today. In summer and in winter, the Beethoven House at Heiligenstadt is now one of the most popular "Heuriger" of Vienna.

The roof of Vienna's famous St. Stephen's Cathedral is itself a symbol of the fusion of new and old which makes up the Austria of today. The coat-of-arms traced out in coloured tiles on the side of the roof shown here are those of the Habsburg dynasty with whom, for more than 600 years, Austria's triumph and tragedy as an empire were shared. But on the other side are shown the arms of the young Austrian Republic together with those of the City of Vienna.

Twice in its long history the great cathedral has been gutted. The original 12th century edifice was almost completely burnt down in 1258. The construction of the main features of the present Gothic building stretched from 1304 until 1450. A large part of this, one of the most beautiful cathedrals of the Middle Ages, was destroyed in April 1945 when, during the last days of fighting in the capital, sparks from blazing houses nearby set fire to scaffolding around the cathedral's tower and roof.

The whole of Austria contributed to the rebuilding of the capital's main landmark. The province of Lower Austria provided the new flooring; Upper Austria the new great bell; Styria the great gate; Carinthia the chandeliers; Tyrol the glass windows; Vorarlberg the pews; Burgenland the marble communion bench; Salzburg the tabernacle; and Vienna the roof. It was a day of national rejoicing when, in April 1952, the cathedral, rebuilt for the second time in its history, was complete again.

This panorama of Vienna is taken from the tower of St. Stephen's Cathedral. It is a vantage point 450 feet above the ground which has been put to many uses since the original tower was completed in 1433. For centuries, it was the main military look-out of the capital. It was from here that emergency light signals were flashed when the Turks closed in on the capital in the 17th century, and it was from here that the advance of the first relief columns was observed.

When the days of land sieges passed away, St. Stephen's spire became the highest observation point of Vienna's fire service. The fireguard post, which was sited just over halfway up the spire, was only dissolved in 1955.

The view shown here also spans the centuries. In the left foreground is St. Peter's Church, built by the great baroque architect Fischer von Erlach on the site of an earlier church dating from the 8th century. In the background are the twin towers of the Votiv Church, erected in the 19th century in memory of the Emperor Franz Joseph's escape from an attempted assassination in 1853. And on the extreme right of the picture is one of the largest modern buildings of post-war Vienna, the so-called "Ring Tower" which was finished in 1954.

For all its richness, this ornamental bowl from the Art Museum of
Vienna is a modest example of the capital's treasures. Quite apart
from the world-famous picture galleries, Vienna has the largest collection
of drawings in the world (the Albertina with over 1,000,000 items);
one of the most important Egyptian collections in existence; as well as
many specialized treasures such as collections of old ceramics; arms
and armour; musical instruments; coins; historical carriages; and wall
tapestries.

Nor is science neglected. Vienna also houses one of the greatest collections
of plants and minerals in Central Europe, and the Technical Museum
counts among its exhibits the first petrol-driven car of the world, constructed in Vienna in 1875.

Above all, it possesses in the collection of crown and state treasures
(the so-called Schatzkammer) something unique not only in its beauty
and variety. There is no more complete assembly of crown jewels in
existence, and none which symbolizes so faithfully the whole history
of a people for over a thousand years.

This little country-house on the edge of the Vienna Woods has been chosen as typifying the so-called "Biedermeier Age" in which it was built—that period of peace and false security which stretched between the end of the Napoleonic wars and the national uprisings of 1848.
The comfort and extravagance which were among its main characteristics are both reflected in this extraordinary house—built in 1810 in a carefree mixture of Gothic and oriental styles by an Austrian banker named Geymüller who had made his fortune in the Napoleonic era. A fitting tenant was soon found to match its oriental exterior. During the Congress of Vienna in 1815 the envoy of Turkey was lodged here, and it was in this year that the house acquired its private mosque.
The fortunes of Baron Geymüller did not even last as long as the brief Biedermeier age itself. His heir and nephew got through the money in record time and became the inspiration of Raimund's wellknown comedy "The Spendthrift".

The rich and unspoilt Burgenland, of which a typical harvest scene is shown here, is the most easterly of Austria's provinces and the most recently acquired. Parts of it belonged to the Habsburg empire for two hundred years between the 15th and 17th centuries, but it was not until 1921 that the young Austrian Republic won the province as it now exists from neighbouring Hungary. Border skirmishes as well as a three-year diplomatic tussle were needed to end the dispute. Even then, all four "Burgen", or fortresses, from which the area originally got its name (Pressburg, Ödenburg, Wieselburg, Eisenburg) remained in Czech or Hungarian hands.

But though the Burgenland is young as an Austrian province, it is the most ancient of all Austro-Germanic colonizing areas. It was here that over eleven hundred years ago Charlemagne established Franconian settlers in a feudal mark set for defence purposes on the borderline of the Teuton and Slav worlds. And ever since, these cornfields have been the highway for invading armies from the East.

This glimpse of a vineyard in Lower Austria symbolizes one of the province's many sources of wealth and principal claims to fame. Lower Austria is the geographical and historical heart of the country, since it was around this fertile area north and south of the Danube that the Austrian state had its origin in the feudal mark of the Babenbergers, a thousand years ago.

The region has always been famous for the quality and variety of its wines. One of the principal wine-growing areas lies north of the river and has been popularly known for centuries as the "Wine Quarter".

But though the vineyards are the most picturesque among the natural riches of Lower Austria, they cannot compare in economic importance with the great oilfields in the plains of the Marchfeld east of Vienna. With their annual output of over 3,5 million tons, they have turned Austria into Europe's second oil producing country, surpassed only by Rumania in quantity. It was on the plains where the oil derricks now rise that the founder of Imperial Austria's greatness, Rudolf of Habsburg, laid down the political and military basis for his dynasty with his defeat of the Bohemian King Ottokar in 1278. It was on the same plains that, over 500 years later, Austrian armies successfully challenged the might of Napoleon.

Culturally as well as geographically, the Burgenland is a transition ground between the Alps of Central Europe and the great plains of the East. This Burgenland village scene, with its low-slung houses and its goose-pond, already brings the atmosphere of the Hungarian "puszta".

But the most remarkable natural phenomenon of the province is undoubtedly Lake Neusiedl, which, over twenty miles long and some five miles wide, straddles the Austro-Hungarian border. Though it is the largest of Austria's lakes, it is nowhere much more than three feet deep and can be waded through in calm weather with comfort. The birdlife of the lake is as unique as its other properties, and species are found on its shores which are unknown anywhere else in Europe.

The province is also of considerable sociological interest. Its mixed population typifies the tolerant fusion of races and creeds which characterizes Austria as a whole. Of its 300,000 inhabitants, roughly 40,000 are Croats and over 10,000 Magyars, and there is a strong Protestant element among the predominantly Catholic population. But, in less than two generations, these different strands have been woven into the single thread of a harmonious Austrian province.

This tiny town on the shores of Lake Neusiedl, with little more than 1,500 inhabitants, has become famous for two things—its wine and its storks. The quality of the neighbouring vineyards was established in the Middle Ages, and in 1364 the people of Rust were given the right to seal wine barrels with the municipal coat-of-arms.

The stork-life of the town is one of the most famous natural curiosities of Austria. There is scarcely a roof-top in the town without the strange silhouette of a stork's nest.

The so-called "Humpback World" (Bucklige Welt), a stretch of which is shown here, belongs to the most peaceful and unspoilt of Austria's many undiscovered regions. Geologically, this area 50 miles south of Vienna is one of the last connecting links joining the Central Alpine Massif to its final spurs in the Rosalien and Leitha mountains which overlook the Hungarian plain. Though the Humpback World can boast some respectable peaks over 5,500 feet high, its main characteristic is this open and softly rounded hill country which is found relatively seldom in the Austrian landscape. Its quiet beauty has inspired many writers, including Austria's national poet Anton Wildgans.

A feature of this countryside is that, despite its proximity to the capital, it has the sparse population and untouched natural calm of the most remote alpine region. The small towns and villages hidden in the folds of these hills are favourite inexpensive holiday centres for the Viennese in both summer and winter. The area also contains pilgrimage centres, such as St. Corona, which are of more than local renown.

28

Bernstein Castle in the southern Burgenland. However idyllic it appears on this picture, this 13th century fortress has had anything but an idyllic past. Since the early Middle Ages it formed one of the principal strongpoints in the long chain of forts built to guard the Austrian land from invasions across the eastern plains. Bernstein itself, though besieged by Mongols, Magyars and Turks, and involved in countless minor actions, never surrendered. Its banners are still preserved in the armoury of the castle, which is now adapted for use as a country-house hotel.

This curiously built baroque church in Eisenstadt, provincial capital of the Burgenland, has held the tomb of the great Austrian composer Joseph Haydn since 1820, and is popularly known as "the Haydn Church". Though Haydn was born on the border of the adjoining province of Lower Austria, his name is most closely associated with Eisenstadt since it was at the Palace of the Esterhazys, only a few hundred yards away from this church, that he worked between 1761 and 1790 as house conductor and composer to the Prince. It was here that many of his most famous works were written, and the operas and concerts of the Palace helped to create the reputation of Eisenstadt as "the Versailles of the East".

In June 1954, Eisenstadt was the scene of a Haydn occasion that was both gruesome and touching. The skull of the composer, which had been removed from the grave soon after his burial by misguided admirers, was finally reunited, after nearly 150 years of separation, with the composer's other remains. A long motorcar cavalcade, mainly in mourning but partly in celebration, crawled at a funereal pace from Vienna to Eisenstadt for the ceremony.

The old town of Eisenstadt overlooks the unbroken stretch of the Hungarian plain and, since prehistoric times, fortifications have been built on the site. The town was made the capital of the Burgenland after the loss of Oedenburg (Sopron) to Hungary in 1921.

The Rax and Schneeberg mountains (each well over 6000 feet high) shown on this panorama belong to the chain of Vienna's "backgarden peaks" which rises less than 60 miles south-east of the capital. Though they are equipped with everything the foreign tourist needs, from Alpine rest huts to large luxury hotels, it is primarily as the weekend and holiday playground of the Viennese that these mountains are known. They provide the capital not only with its nearest high mountain air but also with Vienna's water supply, renowned for its quality. The springs which feed the water pipes down to the capital rise in the area shown on this picture.

Nearby is the Semmering pass (3000 feet high), the natural watershed between the Vienna Basin and the neighbouring province of Styria, and, for centuries, a vital link in the trade route connecting the Austrian capital with the Adriatic sea.

It was here that, in 1728, a new pass road was built in the record time of 48 days, to facilitate the journey made in June of that year to Fiume by the Emperor Charles VI. Seventy years earlier, when his predecessor had travelled across the mountain to take the homage of the Styrian nobility, 3000 oxen were needed to pull the carriages over the primitive road. The new pass could be negotiated "with comfort in a twohorse carriage".

The Semmering is also the site of Europe's first mountain railway. It was completed in 1854 under the direction of the Austrian engineer Karl von Ghega, who pushed through his plan despite the ridicule of most railway experts of the day, including the famous Stevenson in England. For six years, 4000 workers laboured through four million working days to build the three miles of tunnels and viaducts needed to scale the height. At its inauguration, the Semmering railway was one of the most progressive engineering feats of its day, and it will always remain one of the most difficult and daring.

This traditional national costume from Lower Austria is that of a winegrower in the Wachau Valley. It is only one of sixty or seventy distinctive national costume forms which still exist in Austria; and to these basic types must be added countless variations, with subtle changes not only from valley to valley, but from village to village.

Nearly all of these genuine costumes are accurate reproductions of the peasant festival dress of former centuries. The further west one goes in Austria, the older these costumes seem to be in origin. Most of those from the Danube Valley, for example, (like this one with its characteristic golden head-dress) date from the early 19th century. In Tyrol and parts of the Salzburg province, costumes from the 18th century are not uncommon. In the great Bregenz forest of Austria's westernmost province of Vorarlberg, costumes even survive in their original 16th century form.

It should be noted that many items of Austrian national dress commonly thought to be traditional are, in fact, relatively recent innovations, largely influenced by the modern world of fashion. To these belong, in its current form, the so-called "dirndl" of the Salzburg province.

Much that is typically Austrian finds expression in these costumes, whether old or new—the warmth of the land, the astounding variety and tenacity of its local traditions, the pride of the people in them, and the legendary charm of Austria's womenfolk.

The majestic Abbey of Melk, whose towers rise over 350 feet above the Danube, is not only one of the largest and loveliest of all baroque buildings in Central Europe. Its own history symbolizes the triumphs and tragedies of the Austrian people over the last 1,000 years. The original edifice is thought to have been built as a castle for the Babenberg dynasty as long ago as the last quarter of the 10th century. About one hundred years later, it was handed over by the same ruling house to the Benedictine monks from St. Lamprecht, and its long history as an Abbey began.

But this transfer from temporal to spiritual hands did not spare the building from the military perils of the Middle Ages. Already in the 14th century it had been reconstructed as a powerful fortress, and few armies who moved up the central Danube valley passed it by. In 1683 it was besieged by the same Turkish army which tried in vain to take Vienna. It was a fire which finally destroyed the original structure, however, and the building as we see it now was constructed on the same site by the famous architect Jakob Prandtauer between the years 1701 and 1738. The two western towers which overlook the river were added last of all by a pupil of Prandtauer's.

Even in its new ecclesiastical form, the Abbey of Melk was destined to play its part in most of the great campaigns of imperial Austria. It was here, for example, in 1805 and again in 1809 that Napoleon resided during both of his advances on the Austrian capital.

The Kuenringer "Danube pirates", who ruled Duernstein from the 12th century, would have remained an obscure feudal family had not one of their chiefs, Hadmar II, gone down in history as goaler to the captive Richard Lionheart of England. It was here that the English king, captured near Vienna on his return from the Crusades, was imprisoned in 1192 while the English collected the ransom demanded by Leopold of Austria for his freedom.

Duernstein is another of the many Danube edifices to bear the full brunt of the campaigns which swept over Austria. In March 1645, during the 30-Years-War, the original building was reduced to a ruin by Swedish troops, and has never been rebuilt since. All that remains today of King Richard's prison are the outer ramparts and a jagged remnant of the keep, silhouetted against the horizon. But the town itself was destined to see further battles. It was near Duernstein that, in November 1805, the allied armies of imperial Austria and Russia scored one of their triumphs against Napoleon's troops.

The Wachau valley, of which Duernstein is one of the venerable jewels, is unquestionably the most beautiful stretch of the Austrian Danube. Its vineyards which stretch through almost every village from Krems to Melk, are among the most renowned in the country. The valley is at its loveliest when a carpet of apricot blossom stretches down, every spring, from the hills to the banks of the river. So many thousands of Viennese and foreign visitors now make their spring-time pilgrimage to the Wachau to see this sight that the narrow twisting road of the valley became incapable of taking the traffic. A new and modern highway—called the "Wine Road"—is now being built, which will run also through Duernstein.

The village of St. Wolfgang on the Upper Austrian lake of the same name was a goal of pilgrims long before it became a goal for tourists. According to local legend, it was the holy Wolfgang, Bishop of Regensburg, who built the original church here with his own hands, and released a healing spring from the ground underneath it.

The present parish church of St. Wolfgang contains one of the finest pieces of Gothic carving in existence—the famous altar screen created by Michael Pacher in the late 15th century. This little church also boasts other notable altar pieces from the 17th and early 18th centuries.

Medieval documents show that pilgrimages to St. Wolfgang were already flourishing in the 14th century. Its fame as a holiday centre, on the other hand, dates from the last 50 years. The symbol of its touristic importance is the "White Horse Inn" on the shores of the lake, whose name has been carried by operettas to all corners of the earth.

St. Wolfgang is in the centre of the Salzkammergut group of lakes. The Schafberg peak, shown rising above it on this picture, is well over 5,300 feet high but can be comfortably reached by Austria's oldest cog-wheel railway. The panorama from the top takes in not only the whole Salzkammergut region but also the mountains of Styria to the south, the plains of Bavaria to the west, and the Czech mountains of the Böhmerwald to the north.

The Mondsee, 15 miles east of Salzburg, is one of the warmest and the quietest of the famous chain of lakes which run through the Salzkammergut.

Since prehistoric times, men have sought rest and shelter under the gigantic "Dragon's Wall" shown on this picture—a face of rock which rises sheer from the blue waters. Traces still survive of lake-dwellings built on stilts on these shores some two thousand five hundred years before Christ. Even the lake's name is surrounded with legend. According to one version, it was called "Moon Lake" because, in the 8th century, the local ruler Duke Odilo II lost himself while hunting at night behind the rock-face and was only saved from plunging to his death in the lake by the moon suddenly breaking through the clouds. A more prosaic explanation is that both lake and village got their name through being used as a post station (Mansio) in Roman times.

There is, however, nothing legendary about ecclesiastical importance of Mondsee. Its famous abbey was a centre of learning and religion for a thousand years after its foundation in 748 by monks from Monte Cassino in Central Italy. Mondsee's attractions for the modern tourist in search of simplicity and peace are equally well-founded.

41

The history of the Abbey of Kremsmuenster stretches back beyond the six centuries of Habsburg rule and beyond even the dynasty of the Babenbergs which preceded them. The original abbey was founded in the eighth century by Tassilo Duke of Bavaria and shows traces of the colonization of Austria by missionary monks from Ireland in the early Dark Ages.

It was built in its present form in the late 17th and early 18th century by Jakob Prandtauer, the architect of Melk. Like Melk, it did long service as a fortress as well as an abbey before assuming its peaceful baroque identity. Though the abbey is ancient, its abbots have kept up with the times. The present building possesses an observatory and is the seat of a wellknown ecclesiastical college.

Few Austrian towns present such a happy combination of the beautiful and the useful as this Upper Austrian city on the river Enns. Its old buildings are a pleasing mixture of late Gothic, Renaissance, and baroque styles. But though the unspoilt atmosphere of the city is almost medieval, its function as the seat of Austria's greatest car industry is highly utilitarian. This industrial tradition stretches back unbroken to the earliest Christian times. Iron was worked here even in the days of the Roman occupation. In the 13th century, an Imperial Privilege gave Steyr the right to have all the iron ore and timber from the nearby iron mountain offered first for public sale on its market square for the space of three days. The locksmiths, armourers, and cutlers of the city exploited this privilege to build up an industry which flourished unchallenged throughout the Middle Ages.

Steyr was threatened in the 16th century by Turkish invaders, and barely was that threat repulsed when the town was ravaged by the wars of religion. The 30-Years-War and the Napoleonic campaigns also took their toll of the city, and it was in the house of the "Lion Apothecary" that the armistice of Christmas Day 1800 was signed between Austria and France.

Yet throughout this troubled history the ancient iron industry of the town kept functioning—now wilting, now flourishing. Finally, in 1869, the "Austrian Manufacturing Company" was founded, to complete the town's transition into the modern industrial age. The present Steyr-Daimler-Puch company, through it has abandoned armaments production for that of motor vehicles, still continues in the 20th century the thousand-year-old iron working tradition of the town.

43

Graz, the beautifully situated capital of Styria, is a good example of a major Austrian town which has preserved something of the charm and intimacy of more leisured days despite its position as one of the political, strategic, and economic centres of the country.

This peaceful view, for example, is taken from one of the main squares in a bustling city of over 226,000 inhabitants. The clock tower, which crowns the Schlossberg-hill in the background, has dominated the panorama of the city ever since its construction in 1561. The great bell alongside it has been tolling for the people of Graz on days of festival or in times of danger ever since it was cast in 1587.

In modern times, Graz has not contented itself with keeping up with events but has marched ahead of them, especially in the fields of commerce and learning. Its university boasts four Nobel Prize winners. Its Technical College has produced two scientists of European renown. Its spring and autumn trade fairs are Austrian's main link with the traditional markets of South East Europe.

Eggenberg Castle near Graz owes its creation in the seventeenth century to a phenomenon which was rare for those times. It was built by Johann Ulrich von Eggenberg who, despite his bourgeois ancestry from a merchant's family at Radkersburg, achieved the highest noble rank of Prince of the Empire in 1623 for services to the Habsburg dynasty. Two years later, he built this castle as his seat.

Though he could not quite keep up with the current mode of kings and have a room for every day of the year, he did his best to build on the grand scale by having exactly 365 windows put into the castle. But the family of Eggenberg was not destined to survive long after reaching the apex of its remarkable career. In 1755, the male line died out, and the castle passed into other hands.

Styria is above all the province of the hunter. It is therefore fitting that this, the most important castle of the provincial capital, should even today be a museum of the shoot and the chase.

The weirdly beautiful "Ore Mountain" of Styria is the biggest mineral treasure of Austria after the oilfields of the eastern plains. But unlike the oilfields, whose discovery and exploitation was left till the 20th century, the industrial history of the Ore Mountain dates from the beginning of Christian times.

The profile of the mountain is a strange combination of prehistoric nature and centuries of man's activity. Originally, 60 great steps, each nearly 40 feet high, were cut into its side. Today, these have been reduced to the 30 giant shelves shown on the picture, each over 70 feet high, and more than 700 yards long.

The flourishing and progressive iron industry which now works the mountain's treasures has been nationalized since the end of the Second World War. It operates without the fear that its precious source will run out in the near future. The reserves of the Ore Mountain are still estimated at about 330 million tons. At the current excavation rate of some 2,5 million tons a year, this is enough to keep the blast furnaces of Austria fully working for well over another 100 years.

This mountain typifies a phenomenon rare in the Machine Age. Like the great factories which encircle it, it blends happily into the landscape, with an artificial grandeur of its own. Austria is lucky enough to have a heavy industry in her economy without a Black Country on her landscape.

The Styrian paper-making town of Frohnleiten, on the banks of the swiftly running river Mur between Bruck and Graz, is yet another of those examples of Austrian provincial industrial centres which have preserved both their historic character and their beautiful natural setting.

The migration of cattle up to the "Almen", or mountain pastures, in spring, and their return to the valleys in autumn are among the most picturesque sights which Austrian country life has to offer. Both are great days in the annual calendar of the villagers, and both are celebrated with a strong dash of ancient superstition as well as traditional custom.

The "Auftrieb", or procession up to the pastures, is normally held towards the end of March on the lower slopes, from where, about the middle of June, the cattle are taken to the highest pastures. Certain days, such as a Friday or Sunday, are considered incorrect or unlucky. Before the cattle leave their sheds in the village, the old Christian ceremony of protecting them from mishap on their journey is still widely observed. They are given a last meal of sanctified Christmas bread, and touched with holy willows. Even the loud cracking of whips which accompanies the beasts on their climb is not designed to drive them forward by force, but is rather a ceremonial affair dating from heathen recipees for scaring away evil spirits.

The "Abfahrt", or procession down from the alpine pastures, can take place any time up to the end of September. This is an occasion for general rejoicing. The last week before the descent, the so-called "Schoppwoche", is traditionally devoted in all the alpine huts to singing, dancing and drinking. The last night on the mountains before the move (in Tyrol called the "Grünnacht", or green night) forms the climax at which the celebrations last from dusk till early dawn, when the cattle are set moving.

Though the picture opposite is a modest example, such processions can often be very elaborate. The men and women who have attended the herds throughout the summer months put on their finery. The leading cow wears an enormous bell around its neck and often carries on its horns a head-dress of golden tinsel and glass pearls. The other cattle are given little wreaths of alpine flowers.

Once the procession gets safely down to its home village, it is greeted with music and the characteristic blank rounds of mortar fire which accompany most alpine celebrations. This, however, can only take place if no mishap has overtaken the herd during its pasturing time. If one of the animals should have died, or a disease have broken out, the celebrations are cancelled, and special mourning wreaths of deep violet and black are hung on the returning cattle.

Behind all this maze of tradition and superstition there are the practical outlines of a highly important agricultural activity. Austria's milk cows alone number well over a million head, and their milk production in 1955 was over 2,5 million tons.

This Christmas fir tree, whose lights shine in a snow-covered Salzburg landscape, expresses what is a relatively modern tradition. Illuminated Christmas trees are first mentioned around the year 1600 in Central Europe, but the customs from which they derive go back much further. The ceremony is allegedly a survival of the heathen belief that the new life energy developed after midwinter by all trees and bushes should be carried into people's homes to radiate its power among all who dwell there.

Relics of this older belief are still to be observed in many a peasant house of the Austrian countryside, where sprigs of fir or pine trees are nailed over the door or hung over portraits of the Holy Family in the living room.

It was at Oberndorf, an old settlement of boatmen on the river Salzach, not far from these mountains, that the world's most famous Christmas song was composed. On Christmas Eve of the year 1818, the village organist Franz Gruber and his friend the priest Josef Mohr respectively composed the music and words of "Silent Night, Holy Night". The little church of St. Nikolaus where the song was first played, no longer stands. But the song will last as long as Christmas itself.

The origins of the famous Salzburg spa of Bad Gastein are another charming mixture of legend and fact. The local folklore has it that the warm healing springs of the town were discovered in 1680 by hunters pursuing a wounded stag. The documentary history of the springs dates from the 14th century, and among the first of the spa's many prominent guests was the later German Emperor Frederick III, who visited the springs in 1436 shortly before his ascent to the throne.

Gastein, as the world knows it today, was built up largely in the 19th century when its waters —a combination of temperature and radio-activity unique in the world—attracted the sick and the prominent from all continents.

In recent years, the spa has also developed into a winter sports centre of the first rank. A cable railway and many ski-lifts have been built on the surrounding mountains, and it has become the venue of international championships.

The so-called "Perchten", shown climbing through the snow in the foreground of this picture, give a typically Austrian contrast of old with new. With their weird head-dresses, bells and chains, they symbolize, among other things, the coming forces of spring, and their noisy race down the hills every January 6th is one of the most picturesque sights of the Salzburg province.

This view of Salzburg shows the fortress, the old landmark of the town and surrounding countryside, towering over the festival theatre, the 20th century centre of the city's musical life.

The music festivals themselves are, however, older than is generally supposed. They date from 1842, when the Salzburg memorial for Mozart was unveiled. The International Mozart Foundation was constituted already in 1870, and the construction of the Mozarteum Music Conservatory was begun in 1910. But it was only in the 1920s, under the inspiration of men like Max Reinhardt and Hugo von Hofmannsthal, that the festivals developed into red-letter days in the world's calendar of culture.

Though Mozart was born in a house a few hundred yards from the scene of this picture, he spent only part of his working life in the service of the Prince-Archbishops who ruled Salzburg in his day. In 1777, at the age of 21, he left their employment temporarily, and, four years later, severed all permanent connections.

The flourishing city of Salzburg is the capital of the Austrian province of the same name. Today, its principal source of income is the tourist trade, which reaches a hectic peak with the five weeks of the festival season.

52

AUSTRIA, BY AUSTRIA'S GREATEST POET

(Franz Grillparzer, 1791—1872)

". . . It is a goodly land
Well worth a kingly venture.
Where did you ever see its match?
Look round about: wher'ere the eye may rest
It laughs as the bride does to her lover;
With luscious green and meadows flow'r-beset,
Embroidered blue and yellow with flax and saffron fields,
Its mellow air perfumed with herbs—
A nosegay, wreathed by the Danube's silver.
Gaily the valleys broad stretch up
To hillocks, where the generous sun
Casts golden burnish on the juicy grape.
The hunter's realm, dark forests, crowns the whole;
And God's mild breath that hovers over it
Warms and ripens and makes the pulses throb
As in the frozen steppes they never will.
Thus is the Austrian gay and frank:
Owns willingly his faults, and never hides his joy;
Envies not, lets others envy him . . .
Oh goodly land! Oh fatherland!
Twixt Italy the child and manly Germany
Thou liest—a red-cheeked stripling.
May God preserve thy youthful heart,
May he redress what other hands have spoiled".

(English translation by J. H. Blumenthal, 1931)

If Salzburg's music festivals have a drawback, it is that they sometimes tend to obscure the city's claim to fame in its own right. For even had W. A. Mozart never been born in the narrow Getreidegasse, Salzburg would surely have won international renown as one of the world's loveliest cities.

A good idea of its concentrated beauty is given in these two views of the Cathedral square. In one, the misty silhouette of the 900-year-old fortress is shown against a foreground of colonnades. The other shows a close-up of the "Immaculata" statue, a symposium of lead-moulded figures erected in 1771.

Many of the town's most beautiful buildings arose in the first half of the 17th century, and it is from this period that the famous Cathedral also dates. It was constructed between 1614 and 1628 by Santino Solari on the site of an 8th century basilica.

It is in this square that the open-air performances of the morality play "Everyman" are held during the festival season. The anonymous play, whose English text dates from the first half of the 16th century, was first performed in this natural setting in 1920, and has ever since remained a standard feature of the festival programme. The dramatic highpoint of this particular production of the work are the invisible admonishers whose voices sound out from the facade of the Cathedral and even from the parapets of the fortress high above.

Austria's southern most province of Carinthia is not only a borderland between two states. In culture, climate, landscape, and population it is a transition ground between Central Europe and the Italian and South Slav worlds.

This view of the Drau river valley, which runs west to east across the province not far from the Italian and Jugoslav frontiers, typifies this characteristic. There is still a strong reminder of the Alpine theme which dominates the Austrian countryside. But the open and friendly fields in the foreground give a strong hint of the sun-drenched Italian South which lies only a few miles off.

Carinthia's role as a crucible of nature makes it one of the richest and most versatile of the Austrian provinces. Apart from timber, there are large deposits of coal, magnesite, lead and zinc ore, and its rivers and mountains supply an important and steadily expanding hydro-electric industry. The landscape—and particularly the many lakes—guarantee a constant stream of tourists and holiday-makers, while Carinthia's position on the age-old trade route between Vienna and Venice gives it permanent importance as a communications link.

Carinthia gets its name from the Celtic race of the Carnians who were absorbed in the Roman Empire at the beginning of the Christian era. The region flourished under Roman rule as one of the chief centres of the iron industry of Noricum, as Roman Austria was called.

Remarkable fresh evidence of this Roman civilization has been brought to light since the Second World War by the important excavations carried out by the Provincial Government on the Magdalensberg, a rise near the old Carinthian town of St. Veit. The work so far carried out is enough to show that this was a Roman settlement of considerable importance, which served less as a military fortress than as a peaceful provincial centre. Public interest in these discoveries has been so great that a new motor road has been built to link this and other inaccessible sights of Carinthia to the main north-south route.

Hochosterwitz Castle in Carinthia is, in its romantic style, one of the loveliest in Austria. It is one of the few still to remain in possession of the original owners—the Khevenhüller family who built it in the second half of the 16th century. It is also unusual in that it was never submitted to a major siege though, in the times of the second Turkish invasion, it gave asylum to many of the local people. This relatively untroubled history is partly due to its construction which would daunt the heart of the fiercest invader—14 successive castle gates and many bastions guarding the steep ascent to the summit of the limestone peak on which it was built. But, as its relatively recent origin shows, the castle itself dates from the era when these massive stone dwellings were already losing their importance as fortresses and becoming instead ornate places of residence.

This picture of sunset over Lake Wörther, with its almost tropical blaze of colours, shows how strongly the influence of the South pervades the Carinthian atmosphere.

The Wörthersee is the largest and most frequented of the 200 odd lakes which are dotted all over the province. Its busiest tourist centres are Pörtschach and Velden, and the whole of the socalled "Austrian Riviera" which stretches between. Here, all the sophisticated apparatus of an international holiday region has been created—flower carnivals, "concours d'élegance" for fashions and automobiles, roulette casinos, major tennis tournaments, and numberless congresses. This northern coast of the lake is doubly busy since, in addition to its tourist attractions, it lies on the main road and rail route between Vienna and Northern Italy.

The southern shores of the lake, though they boast one of the best golf courses in Austria, are on the whole less sophisticated and more idyllic. The picturesque peninsula of Maria Wörth juts out halfway along this southern side—an ancient pilgrimage centre with two old churches, one of which dates from the 10th century.

In temperature as well as in setting, the Wörthersee has a breath of the warm South. Bathing can often go on comfortably until well into the autumn, at a time when the lakes of northern Austria are only for the hardiest fanatic.

Heiligenblut in Western Carinthia is the picturesque gateway to the great Grossglockner road, one of the most modern alpine pass routes in Central Europe. The sharp snow-covered peak of the Grossglockner towers up in the background. Nearly 12,500 feet high, it is the highest of all Austria's countless mountains. It was first scaled in the year 1800 by a village priest from the East Tyrol. Today, the whole region around the peak and the huge six-mile-long Pasterze glacier below it form a special reservation area for winter sports enthusiasts. The great motor road over the Glockner is some thirty miles long and was built between 1930 and 1935, despite the serious economic troubles which the First Austrian Republic was then facing. Its highest point, the so-called Hochtor, or High Gate, was already used by the Romans as a crossing point of the Tauern Range to which the mountain belongs. Despite its inevitable associations with the Grossglockner road, Heiligenblut is an Austrian beauty spot in its own right. Its name comes from a local legend that some of the holy blood of Christ was brought here for preservation.

Lake Millstatt, in the centre of the province, is one of the most peaceful of the larger Carinthian lakes, despite its accessibility on the main east-west route from Lienz to Klagenfurt, the provincial capital. Long stretches of its shores are unspoilt and unbuilt-upon, like the section shown in this view. Yet the increasing flow of tourists and holiday-makers is forcing Millstatt to adopt more and more of the up-to-date methods used by its sophisticated sisters like Lake Wörther. And nearby, at Radenthein, lies an ever-expanding centre of Austria's magnesite production.

The lake itself is the bed of an Ice-Age glacier stream which ran here between two wooded peaks on the southern edge of the Tauern Range. Though more than 1800 feet high, the climate of the lake is remarkably mild.

Among the main sites of the town of Millstatt is a former Benedictine monastery with an 11th century church and a lime-tree one thousand years old in its ground.

The ancient lime-tree typifies the age-old history of the Millstatt area as a cultural settlement. Celtic and other remains which have been dug up from the banks of the lake show that pre-Christian peoples sougth shelter on these shores. Roman graves have also been found here to testify to the part Millstatt already played at a time when most of present-day Austria was one of the northern bastions of the Roman Empire.

The connected and documented history of the villages on the lake is as old as the town of Millstatt itself, and suggests that by the early Middle Ages a flourishing community existed all around these shores.

The Dolomite mountains of Lienz, shown here in midwinter, are one of the many grandiose chains which dominate the landscape of the East Tyrol region. These peaks, known in local dialect as "The Monsters", are the most easterly spurs of the Italian Dolomite range.

Until 1918, the present areas of North, East, and South Tyrol were one united Austrian province. The transfer of the South Tyrol to Italy after the First World War severed all common boundaries between the other two parts.

The East Tyrol is today one of the most peaceful as well as most beautiful of all Austria's mountain regions, having remained outside the main stream of tourist traffik.

Few things express more strikingly the deep religious sense which characterizes the people of Tyrol than these socalled "Marterle", which can be found dotted on pathways and peaks all over the mountains of the province.

Strictly speaking, they are burial or memorial signs for ordinary persons who died or were killed by accident on the spot marked. In this form, they usually countain a picture of the deceased, with the details of his death and the request that passers-by should pray for his soul.

In a broader sense, these "Marterle" are simply wooden or stone posts carrying a holy picture, or else crucifixes or small religious statues which still fall short of a mountain chapel proper.

The word almost certainly derives in some form from "martyr" or "martyria".

The Virgen Valley, which lies well over 3,000 feet high in the East Tyrol, is typical of scores in the province—a gently sloping basin of meadows and woods, divided by a mountain stream and leading up on either side to the snow-clad peaks of the Alps.
Characteristic of most of these valleys are the isolated and beautifully tended farmhouses of the local peasants, whose very solitude adds to the tranquillity of the scene. Yet even the remotest of these valleys are often directly linked with the world of great events which seems to have passed them by. Near the village of Hinterbichl, for example, which lies at the end of this particular valley, is situated the summer school of the world-famous Vienna Choir Boys.

The picturesque dress which these villagers from Praegarten in the East Tyrol are wearing is as much of a uniform as an ancient peasant costume: it is the garb of the Tyrolean Riflemen, a self-defence organization formed by the free men of the province in the late Middle Ages. Among the many actions which the ancestors of these villagers fought in these same costumes was the famous rebellion of the Tyrolean peasants against Napoleon under Andreas Hofer in 1809. The proud martial tradition which these costumes express is also a proud democratic one. From the early 15th century, the free citizens and peasants of Tyrol were represented in their provincial diets on an equal footing with the local nobility and clergy.

This palette of contrasting moods and colours shows the range of the Carinthian landscape. In the background, a mountain peak typical of any alpine chain in early spring; in the foreground, a rich mixture of meadow, pine and birch.

The wealth of Carinthia is also shown in this view. Over 40% of the province is forest, and timber is one of its principal products. Here, we are on the lower slopes of the wooded belt, which ends in this part of the Eastern Alps at about 5,500 feet. But there is already enough space for the birch, with its characteristic longing for light and air, to get its head clear.

This panoramic view of Innsbruck, the ancient and lovely capital of the Tyrol, shows many of the historic and natural landmarks of the city. The twin-towered church in the foreground, the socalled Hofkirche, contains what is perhaps the most important German sculpture of the Renaissance period. This is the monument worked in metal for the marble sarcophagus of the great Habsburg Emperor Maximilian I. The church itself was built in 1553-63 to take his tomb, though in fact the ruler was buried in Wiener Neustadt, Lower Austria.

Behind the church is the palace built by Maximilian as his town residence. The documented history of Innsbruck goes back far beyond the Habsburg dynasty. It was first named in records in the early 11th century and was established as a fortified town as early as 1180.

In the background towers the peak of the Patscherkofel mountain, whose rounded cone-shape is one of the rarest sights in an Alpine range. It is a wellknown centre for holidaymakers and tourists in summer and winter alike.

The valley of the Inn, shown here from the village of Mösern, is the largest of all the valleys of Tyrol and, at the same time, the most important communications and industrial artery of the province. In this lovely broad valley are situated not only Innsbruck, the provincial capital, but all the larger Tyrolean towns and the local industries associated with them such as Jenbach (machinery); Wörgl (wood fibre products); Kufstein (metal and timber); Wattens (glass); and Imst, to name only one of the textile centres.

It is from the Inn valley that the narrower side valleys of the Tyrol branch off—like the Oetz, the Ziller, the Stubai and Paznaun valleys, each one a holiday centre in its own right. Parallel to the river run the main road and rails links which connect the Alps to Eastern Europe, and at right angles across the valley run some of the main north-south routes of the Continent. To combine all this activity and all this importance, and yet remain as peaceful and unspoilt as this view suggests, is an Austrian speciality.

70

Though the province of Tyrol is always thought of as a mountain region, it also contains some of Austria's loveliest and most unspoilt lakes. This is one of them—the Achen Lake which lies a few miles north of the main Innsbruck—Wörgl road, to which it is linked by the excellent motor route shown. The lake is some 3,000 feet high and is noted locally for the unusual deep blue of its water.

Nearby are one of Tyrol's oldest castles and one of her newest power plants. Tratzberg Castle already appears in the chronicles of the 13th century and, some 300 years later, it belonged for a time to the Fuggers, the famous German merchant and banking family. The power plant, which is named after the lake, is a major link in Austria's great hydro-electric chain. Thus even near the shores of this idyllic mountain lake, the new and the old of Austria are found close together in a characteristic blend.

71

The Grossvenediger Mountain (just over 12,000 feet) shown on this picture is the second highest peak of Austria, being surpassed only by the Grossglockner, a glimpse of which was given in an earlier scene.

The "Venediger" is one of the finest skiing and climbing mountains in Austria. The ascent can be made via a chain of rest-huts which, outside the great wintersports centres, still form the backbone of the Alpine tourist industry. For the skier, the enormous untracked slopes which lie beneath the peak of the Venediger provide perfect natural deep-snow runs.

The glaciers and streams of this mountain region also form an inexhaustible reservoir for Austria's hydro-electric power plants which are among the greatest in Europe.

72

The mountains of the Ziller Valley, not far from Innsbruck in the Tyrol, crown one of the loveliest and most popular Alpine regions of Austria. The peaks shown are typical of the savage beauty of this range, which contains no fewer than 132 glaciers. They afford many difficult climbs for the enthusiast, and it is on mountains such as these that the climbers of many nations have trained for their conquest of the great peaks of the Himalayas or the Andes.

In autumn, this region is famed for its chamois shooting, and some of the record trophies of the world have been shot in this area of the Alps.

The Ziller Valley itself forms a complete contrast to the lonely severity of these peaks. It is dotted with picturesque villages, whose "Kirchtage", or open-air church festivals, are among the most colourful in the country.

The winter sports centre of Seefeld lies on Austria's most beautiful railway—the Karwendelbahn—which climbs up from Innsbruck, boring through the legendary Martin's Wall on its way. The resort lies some 3900 feet high and, as the picture shows, is perched on a huge plateau between the encircling mountains. Despite the ever increasing number of modern hotels, it is still the 15th century parish church which dominates its attractive silhouette.

The attraction of Kitzbühel, the most famous winter resort of the Austrian Tyrol, is not to be explained simply by its unique "ski-circus" nor by the variety of its lodgings, which range from the simplest pension to the most luxurious international hotel. The secret of its appeal is that, despite the chromium-plated efficiency of modern tourism, it has clung on miraculously to the atmosphere and appearance of a medieval town. This, more than the cable railways and chair lifts, draws year after year its record stream of tourists who outnumber many times over the 7,000 odd residents of the town. Kitzbuehel's happy combination of old and new is well illustrated in this scene. In the upper foreground is the line of the old defence wall, drawn in front of the 500-year-old pencil-spired church. The slit in the mountain wood in the background marks the path of the modern cable railway which leads up to the Hahnenkamm peak.

This view of the Silvretta mountains of the Vorarlberg, with the giant wall of a power dam driven into their side, typifies the union of science and nature, and of old and new, which makes up Austria's westernmost province.

The Silvretta group of the Rhaetian Alps stretches from Switzerland across the Vorarlberg and into the neighbouring province of Tyrol. The chain is studded with peaks over 10,000 feet high and is scored with countless glaciers. Such Alpine regions are the reservoirs of Austria's so-called "white gold" or hydro-electric power.

The construction shown here is part of the Illwerk Power Plant with an annual capacity of some 1,000 million kilowatt hours a year, which is being constantly expanded. In addition to feeding Austria's home needs and enabling projects such as the electrification of the federal railways to be carried out, the hydro-electric industry makes an important contribution to the country's trade balance. The Illwerk, for example, sends over one third of its output to Western Germany.

This plant is one of a gigantic chain constructed or developed throughout the Austrian Alps since the Second World War. The biggest of these projects is that at Kaprun in the Salzburg province. Another important one has been built on the Danube at Ybbs Persenbeug, 60 miles west of Vienna.

In addition to the deliveries to Germany, Austria exports her electric power to most of her other neighbours. Yet all the stations completed and planned do not account for half of the country's hydro-electric potential, which is estimated at the astronomic figure of 40,000 million kilowatt hours a year.

It is difficult to guess from this picture of the beautiful Vorarlberg town of Rankweil that an important regional centre of Austria's textile industry is tucked away between the slopes of the mountains. Yet for all its natural beauty, the province of Vorarlberg, which borders on Switzerland, is relatively the most industrialized in Austria. It is textile plants which form the backbone of this provincial industry, and this fact finds its annual expression in the Trade Fair of Dornbirn, a few miles north-east of Rankweil, which has become one of the leading textile exhibitions of Europe.

In appearance and character, Rankweil is anything but a miniature industrial centre. The 600-year-old Liebfrauen Church dominates the skyline just as serenely as it did in the days when Rankweil was more known for its pilgrimages than for its cloth.

This view of the evening waters of Lake Constance brings us to the westernmost boundary of Austria, and at the same time completes the gamut of variations in the Austrian landscape. For here, though the nearest ocean lies over two hundred miles away, the mood of the open sea is somehow recaptured in the midst of the Alps. The lake's mild climate and the plentiful crops of fruit and wine which grow on its shores help the Mediterranean illusion for the visitor.

Bregenz, on the Austrian shore of the lake, is now noted above all for its summer festivals. Started after the Second World War, these have succeeded in giving a new and picturesque setting to the classical operettas of Vienna. Every year, as the main attraction of the festival, one of these works is performed on a giant floating stage as the so-called "Play on the Lake". Thus, even at the westernmost tip of Austria, the spirit of Vienna is preserved through adaptation.

TECHNICAL DATA

All pictures taken in Agfacolor by Kurt Peter Karfeld and Dr. Irmtraud Karfeld

Page					Page				
15	View of Vienna	F: 9	$1/60$ sec.	2 p. m.	40	St. Wolfgang	F: 6,3	$1/100$ sec.	1 p. m.
20	Cathedral Roof	F: 4,5	$1/200$ sec.	12 noon	50	Christmas Tree	F: 2,3	$1/1$ sec.	5 p. m.
21	View from Cathedral	F: 6,3	$1/50$ sec.	5 p. m.	51	Gastein	F: 12,5	$1/100$ sec.	11 a. m.
17	Belvedere Gate	F: 11	$1/75$ sec.	11 a. m.	52	Festival House	F: 4,5	$1/25$ sec.	6 p. m.
18	Beethoven House	F: 4,5	$1/60$ sec.	4 p. m.	54	Cathedral Square	F: 3,5	$1/30$ sec.	8 a. m.
22	Ornamental Bowl	F: 3,5	$1/15$ sec.		55	Madonna	F: 12,3	$1/25$ sec.	5 p. m.
23	Biedermeier House	F: 9	$1/60$ sec.	10 a. m.	56	Drau Valley	F: 12,5	$1/60$ sec.	10 a. m.
24	Harvest Scene	F: 12,5	$1/100$ sec.	2 p. m.	59	Lake Woerther	F: 3,5	$1/20$ sec.	7 p. m.
26	Farm House	F: 9	$1/60$ sec.	3 p. m.	58	Hochosterwitz	F: 6,3	$1/100$ sec.	12 noon
27	Rust	F: 9	$1/60$ sec.	11 a. m.	61	Heiligenblut	F: 9	$1/60$ sec.	11 a. m.
31	Haydn Church	F: 6,3	$1/60$ sec.	10 a. m.	62	Lake Millstatt	F: 5,6	$1/60$ sec.	4 p. m.
32	Rax Mountain	F: 12,5	$1/50$ sec.	12 noon	68	Mountain Birch	F: 6,3	$1/60$ sec.	5 p. m.
28	"Humpback World"	F: 6,3	$1/50$ sec.	5 p. m.	64	Alpine Crosses	F: 4,5	$1/25$ sec.	7 a. m.
29	Bernstein Castle	F: 9	$1/100$ sec.	11 a. m.	65	Lienz Dolomites	F: 5,6	$1/25$ sec.	10 a. m.
25	Chapel	F: 12,5	$1/60$ sec.	10 a. m.	66	Tyrol Costumes	F: 6,3	$1/100$ sec.	3 p. m.
35	National Costume	F: 5,6	$1/60$ sec.	6 p. m.	67	Virgen Valley	F: 9	$1/60$ sec.	2 p. m.
37	Melk Abbey	F: 9	$1/50$ sec.	5 p. m.	69	Innsbruck	F: 4,5	$1/25$ sec.	6 p. m.
38	Duernstein	F: 9	$1/100$ sec.	11 a. m.	72	Grossvenediger	F: 12,5	$1/100$ sec.	11 a. m.
42	Kremsmuenster	F: 12,5	$1/100$ sec.	1 p. m.	73	Zillertal Alps	F: 9	$1/100$ sec.	3 p. m.
43	Steyr	F: 6,3	$1/60$ sec.	9 a. m.	70	Inn Valley	F: 6,3	$1/100$ sec.	11 a. m.
41	Salzkammergut	F: 12,5	$1/50$ sec.	8 a. m.	71	Lake Achen	F: 6,3	$1/200$ sec.	1 p. m.
44	Graz	F: 6,3	$1/100$ sec.	5 p. m.	74	Seefeld	F: 9	$1/100$ sec.	3 p. m.
45	Eggenberg Castle	F: 9	$1/100$ sec.	11 a. m.	75	Kitzbuehel	F: 12,5	$1/60$ sec.	10 a. m.
47	Erzberg	F: 6,3	$1/60$ sec.	9 a. m.	76	Ill Power Plant	F: 6,3	$1/60$ sec.	3 p. m.
48	Mountain Cattle	F: 9	$1/75$ sec.	12 noon	78	Rankweil	F: 9	$1/60$ sec.	11 a. m.
46	Frohnleiten	F: 9	$1/60$ sec.	11 a. m.	79	Lake Constance	F: 4,5	$1/60$ sec.	5 p. m.